THE
Orchid
Show at The New York Botanical Garden

THE NEW YORK BOTANICAL GARDEN

PHOTOGRAPHS BY JOHN PEDEN

Contents

Opposite: *Paphiopedilum* Lynleigh Koopowitz

Foreword

With more than 30,000 naturally occurring species and tens of thousands of artificially created hybrids, the orchid is the world's largest family of flowering plants. Each year, early in spring, *The Orchid Show* presents more than 5,000 orchids from Africa, Asia, the Americas, and the Caribbean in the galleries of the Garden's landmark Enid A. Haupt Conservatory.

In this book, John Peden's compelling images convey the vibrant beauty, intricate structure, and captivating intrigue of the mesmerizing flowers featured in *The Orchid Show*. His artfully composed photographs capture the beauty and diversity of the orchids themselves. They also display the dramatic exhibition designs and vignettes, new each year, which fascinate *Orchid Show* newcomers and beckon thousands to return annually.

Our deep gratitude goes to The Tiffany & Co. Foundation, sponsors of *The Orchid Show*. Tiffany has had the foresight to recognize the widespread appeal of orchids and the thoughtfulness to appreciate the conservation, environmental, and horticultural messages that orchids can help communicate. The Tiffany & Co. Foundation has also had the generosity to lend handsome support to bring this exhibition to the public.

I hope this lovely book serves as a reminder to come restore your spirits and be inspired by nature at *The Orchid Show*.

Gregory Long

Gregory Long, *President*
The New York Botanical Garden

Opposite: *Renanthera* Brookie Chandler 'Red Devil'

The Orchid Show at The New York Botanical Garden

KIM E. TRIPP, PH.D.

Senior Vice President for Horticulture and Living Collections

Everyone loves orchids—their exotic and primal flowers evoke the strongest passions of any flower we know. *The Orchid Show*, held every year at The New York Botanical Garden as winter gives way to spring, is unique in offering a museum experience of a vast array of glorious flowering orchids presented in a dramatic "living theater." The orchids are displayed in the galleries of the Enid A. Haupt Conservatory in specially created naturalistic habitats. Other specimens—rare flowering rain forest plants, palms, lianas, bromeliads, and ferns—are brought together with the orchids to create realistic settings that evoke the jungles, cloud forests, remote mountains, and dangerous river valleys in which these delicious plants grow. Each year, a brand-new exhibit is created with fresh surprises in plants and plant stories—and, of course, thousands of new orchids!

The orchids among which you can stroll and dream within the beautiful glass galleries of the Conservatory are selected each year to offer the greatest diversity of

different types of orchids of any exhibition in the United States. From the rarest of species orchids carefully selected from the Garden's permanent living collection to cultivated hybrids from the world's most renowned orchid growers and breeders; from delicate miniatures to the extraordinary Darwin's star orchid to orchids which have inspired Tiffany jewels, there is an incredible range on display.

The Orchid Show at the Garden is also unique in offering extensive public education about orchids. Visitors are able to learn about and appreciate their fascinating natural history and ecology, horticultural background, and discover home growing tips and techniques. Informative signs and audio tours explain and interpret the plants and their stories in *The Orchid Show* itself. Workshops and demonstrations, Question and Answer sessions, curator-led tours, and lectures and presentations are offered every day while the show is open to inspire and inform about every aspect of growing, conserving, and studying orchids— including fascinating programs given by the Garden's scientists who study the biology and ecology of the elusive orchid in the wild and the laboratory. In

addition, during the show, the Shop in the Garden offers thousands of beautiful orchids from around the world for sale. These range from easy-to-grow plants for the novice to much more unusual and hard-to-find varieties for the connoisseur.

The Garden has grown orchids in its living plant collections for more than a century for conservation, for study, and for the pure delight of sharing with our visitors the beauty and mystery of these amazing plants. The Garden's orchid collection spends most of its life in the Nolen Greenhouses for Living Collections, where it is developed, propagated, and cared for by expert orchid growers and curators. A number are displayed year-round in the Thekla E. Johnson Orchid Rotunda. But once a year, the orchids are brought to the Conservatory for an extravagant and glorious exhibition. I hope that you will turn the pages of this book to experience again *The Orchid Show* whenever your own love of orchids calls you, and that you will come to experience the treasures of the living orchids at the Garden as winter turns toward spring each year.

pposite: *Odontoglossum triumphans* illustration by Walter Hood Fitch from *A Monograph of Odontoglossum* (1874) by James Bateman.
rom the collections of the LuEsther T. Mertz Library.

11

A Brief Introduction to Orchids

Orchids represent the height of evolutionary success in the plant kingdom. With more than 30,000 naturally occurring species, they are the largest family of flowering plants. Orchids are adaptable, diverse, and grow in almost every habitat—from semi-desert to Arctic tundra—on every continent except Antarctica. They come in an enormous range of sizes, from miniatures with tiny flowers less than 1/16 of an inch in diameter to giants more than 25 feet tall with flower spikes up to 10 feet long. What makes these fascinating and often extraordinarily beautiful plants so successful? Perhaps the main reason is the close relationship they have developed over time with other life forms. Their histories are intricately woven together with those of animals and fungi.

Orchids come in an amazing array of colors and shapes: Some mimic bees, wasps, butterflies, and moths; others have unusual buckets, traps, and trigger mechanisms. These adaptations help insure that insect pollinators visit the flowers. Because orchid flowers have specialized reproductive parts and their pollen is a single mass, individual grains of pollen cannot disperse as with other flowers. As a result, each orchid flower has only one chance to transfer pollen to another flower. Thus orchid flowers have evolved in strange shapes to be able to interact with specific insect pollinators. Some produce a glue-like substance to attach their pollen to an insect's body. Others can shoot their pollen as if from a gun. Still others have floral traps that force insects to pollinate the flowers as they flee. Some entice pollinators with nectar or fragrance, while others trick them by looking like potential mates. One of the most fascinating strategies is seen in orchid flowers that not only mimic female wasps in shape, but also produce a fragrance similar to wasp pheromones. These orchids manage to fool male wasps into copulating with their flowers, thereby insuring pollination. All of these tricks, traps, and disguises enable orchids to transfer pollen from one flower to another.

Once a flower has been pollinated, the orchid forms a fruit that can contain as many as 70,000 or more dust-like seeds. Unlike most other plants, orchid seeds contain no stored food for the tiny plant embryo inside. Most orchid seeds must be infected by a fungus to provide nourishment to the tiny plant as it begins to grow. This is an adaptation that enables orchids to survive in habitats with poor soils, such as bogs, or without soil altogether, attached to trees or other plants. Such orchids are called epiphytes—plants that grow wholly upon another plant, but are not parasitic and depend on the host plant for support rather than nourishment. Other, similar orchids grow without soil on rocks and are called lithophytes. Epiphytes and lithophytes obtain all necessary nutrients from rainwater through their roots. Members of a third category, terrestrial orchids, grow in the earth and obtain their nutrients from the soil. They are able to store nutrients in underground storage organs, such as tubers, corms, or swollen roots.

It was, in fact, the roots of terrestrial orchids in the Mediterranean region that gave rise to the name orchid, which comes from the Greek *orchis*, or testicle, which the tuberous roots of some species resemble. The term was coined in roughly 300 B.C. by the Greek philosopher Theophrastus, known as "the father of botany," in his work *Enquiry into Plants*.

For millennia, humans have appreciated orchids for their beauty and used them for medicine, food, flavoring and perfume. The medicinal use of orchids was discussed in an almost-five-thousand-year-old Chinese text attributed to the legendary emperor Shen Nung. Orchids have also long been cultivated as ornamental plants in both China and Japan; some 2,500 years ago, the Chinese philosopher Confucius called the orchid the "King of Fragrant Plants."

From the days of Theophrastus on, remedies made from orchid parts, usually roots, were included in European books of herbal medicine. Salep, a beverage made from Mediterranean orchid roots, was widely consumed in Europe until coffee replaced it; salep

is still popular in Turkey. Seed pods of *vanilla*, an orchid from tropical America, were first brought to Europe in the early 16th century. The Spanish conquerors of Mexico had found the Aztecs making a drink that combined vanilla with chocolate and chili pepper. Although vanilla was first used in Europe as a fragrance, it later became a popular, though expensive, flavoring. Vanilla is today a very valuable crop.

Until the early 18th century, when European gardeners reportedly began to experiment with their cultivation, the gorgeous flowers of tropical orchids were known in Europe almost exclusively by means of drawings and dried specimens. It was not until the 19th century that tropical orchids began to be cultivated in earnest in Europe and that "orchid-mania" took hold—in England, in particular. 19th-century orchid hunters roamed the forests of distant countries, often risking life and limb, looking for new species to send home. It was not uncommon for exorbitant amounts of money to change hands for unusual specimens, and great strides were made in perfecting orchid cultivation. Today, there is a very significant global trade in cut orchid flowers and cultivated orchid plants. Thailand alone exports more than $250 million worth of cut orchid flowers each year in a world market estimated at $9 billion. In his book *Orchid Fever*, Eric Hanson claims that "more than any other plant under cultivation, orchids have captured the passions of both growers and scientists." In fact, the popularity of orchids is on the rise.

Unfortunately, this popularity may ultimately prove to be the orchid's downfall. Like the elephant, gorilla, and the rhino, wild orchids are under serious threat of extinction from habitat destruction and over-collecting. As with many things in the natural world that are beautiful, the orchid flower tends to be rare and fragile. Perhaps this combination of beauty and vulnerability explains why humans have chosen to immortalize orchids above all other flowers.

Illustrations by Walter Hood Fitch from the collections of the LuEsther T. Mertz Library.
Clockwise from top left: *Odontoglossum roezlii, Anguloa ruckeri, Cattleya dowiana, Houlletia brocklehurstiana*

15

Corsage Orchid   The prominent 19th-century British botanist, horticulturist, and orchid expert John Lindley named the genus *Cattleya* after William Cattley, also an eminent horticulturist and one of the first to create a private orchid collection. *Cattleya* came to England from Brazil in the early 1800s by accident as a part of the protective wrapping for other tropical plants imported by Cattley. He was intrigued by the plant and eventually brought it to flower. It is now one of the most popular orchids among enthusiasts as it is fairly easy to grow and has large, dramatic flowers. Because the flowers make beautiful, long-lasting corsages, it is widely hybridized and grown for its commercial value. There are thousands of hybrids and roughly 60 epiphytic and lithophytic *Cattleya* species in Central and South America.

Opposite: *Cattleya* Clear Morn

CATTLEYA

x *Laeliocattleya* Prism Palette

Asian Corsage Orchid

The name *Cymbidium* is derived from the Greek word for boat and refers to a hollow area in the lip of the flower. There are some 50 terrestrial and epiphytic species ranging from Asia to Australia. These large, showy plants with long leaves and tall spikes of waxy flowers are immensely popular with both orchid enthusiasts and commercial growers. Cymbidiums have been celebrated in Chinese art and literature for thousands of years. Confucius praised their many good qualities and they were written about as a symbol of the perfect personality. The Chinese especially treasured *Cymbidium* plants that had slender, graceful leaves, and modest flowers with an intense perfume. Modern hybrid cymbidiums have much larger leaves and tall spikes of beautiful, long-lasting flowers, but sadly few have the intense fragrance of their wild Chinese ancestors.

Opposite: *Cymbidium* Lingar 'Yellow Alba'

CYMBIDIUM

Clockwise from top left: *Cymbidium* Via Paloma Verde 'Lime Frost', *Blechnum brasiliense*, *Cymbidium* (Via Spring Snow x President Polk) 'Crystal Springs', *Vriesea*

Cymbidium hybrids, *Ludisia discolor*   23

Cane Orchid   *Dendrobium*, aptly named from the Greek *dendron*, tree, and *bios*, life, are epiphytic orchids that have cane-like stems with many joints. This Asian genus is very large and widespread, numbering as many as 1,400 species that grow from India to Japan and south to New Guinea, Tahiti, and Australia. Many species have long been— and still are—used in traditional Chinese medicine. One of the most beautiful, *Dendrobium nobile*, is the main ingredient in *shih-hu*, a Chinese herbal medicine first described more than 2000 years ago. It was recommended as a tonic and strengthening medicine and to promote long life. *Dendrobium* stems have also been used to make baskets and are sometimes cooked with chicken. Because of their long-lasting flowers, dendrobiums are also a major florist crop.

Opposite: *Dendrobium* Salaya Fancy

DENDROBIUM

Clockwise from top left: *Dendrobium* Chasri Gold, *Dendrobium* Suzanne Neil, *Dendrobium* Burana Fancy, *Dendrobium* Burana Sapphire

Clockwise from top left: *Dendrobium spectabile* 'Kokomo', *Dendrobium anosmum*, *Dendrobium* Comet King 'Akatsuki' and Star Sapphire 'KOS', *Dendrobium* Salaya Fancy   27

Reed Orchid

From the Greek *epi*, upon, and *dendron*, tree, *Epidendrum* orchids are, not surprisingly, mostly epiphytic or lithophytic orchids, but may also be terrestrial. They are commonly known as reed orchids because of their long, reed-like stems. The genus was named by the Swedish botanist Linnaeus in his 1740 work *Species Orchidum*, in which he established the first scientific names for orchid genera and species. There are between 500 and 1,000 species of *Epidendrum* that grow in a wide range of habitats and altitudes throughout subtropical and tropical America. Their flowers tend to be small and brightly colored, like the tropical butterflies that pollinate them.

Opposite: *Epidendrum* hybrids

EPIDENDRUM

Pansy Orchid Named for Lord Fitzwilliam Milton, a 19th-century British orchid expert, *Miltonia* was once considered a single genus of about 20 epiphytic species from South America. Now the species have been separated into two genera: *Miltonia* and *Miltoniopsis*. Miltonias grow in low to moderate altitudes in Brazil, while *Miltoniopsis* prefer moderate to high altitudes in the Andean cloud forests of Colombia, Ecuador, and Peru. Both groups like high humidity. *Miltoniopsis* hybrids are becoming increasingly popular because of their large flat flowers, often marked in rich, deep shades of pink and maroon. The charming flower shape and distinctive markings resemble the faces of old-fashioned pansies and give rise to the common name for the genus. Many species of both *Miltonia* and *Miltoniopsis* are sweetly fragrant, with a smell reminiscent of roses or sweet peas.

Opposite: *Miltoniopsis* Maui Star

MILTONIOPSIS

Clockwise from top left: *Miltonia* Herrenhausen, *Miltonia* Keiko Komoda, *Miltonia* Herrenhausen, *Miltonia* Hajime Ono 'Maui Meteor' x 'Maui Mist'

American Moth Orchids

Odontoglossum derives its name from the Greek *odontos*, tooth, and *glossa*, tongue, which refer to a tooth-like callus on their lip. The roughly 100 terrestrial and epiphytic species grow in the cool, wet mountain forests of Central and South America. American moth orchids are considered by many orchid fanciers to be the most dazzling of all orchids and are a genus of great horticultural importance. Their long sprays of flowers look like many colorful moths in flight with spotted and striped wings. Perhaps the most beautiful of all is *Odontoglossum crispum* with white flowers splashed with gold or other colors. European orchid hunters discovered it in 1841, growing high in the Andes. In 1906, a collector paid the equivalent of more than $112,000 in today's currency for a single plant!

Opposite: *Odontoglossum* hybrids

ODONTOGLOSSUM

Ondontocidium Elle's Triumph

x *Vuylstekeara* Cambria 'Noyo'

x *Colmanara* Wildcat 'Ocelot'

Top: x *Odontioda* Red Shine 'Vibrant' x Cherry Glow
Bottom: x *Colmanara* Wildcat 'Chadwick'

38   x *Odontioda* Florence Stirling 'Gina' x Aviewood 'Hawks Hill'

x *Odontioda* Glyndebourne Belmonte

Top: x *Odontioda* Aviewood 'Hawks Hill' x Fort Point 'Gina'
Bottom: *Odontoglossum* Ardentissimum

Dancing Lady Orchids The name *Oncidium* comes from the Greek *onkos*, meaning mass, or body, referring to the wart-like growth on the lip of many species. *Oncidium* is one of the largest genera in the orchid family. Oncidiums can be epiphytic, lithophytic, and occasionally terrestrial, and are found throughout subtropical and tropical America from sea level to high mountain areas. They differ widely in habit, but are easily recognized by their slender branching sprays with many small flowers generally found in shades of yellow and brown. There are hundreds of hybrids among the various species of *Oncidium*, as well as hybrids made with other closely related genera, such as *Odontoglossum*, *Miltonia,* and *Brassia.* These hybrids are highly prized for their long-lasting flowers.

Opposite: *Tolumnia* (formerly *Oncidium*) Golden Sunset 'Waiomao'

ONCIDIUM

Oncidium Sharry Baby 'Taida'   *Oncidium* Saint Dawn Gold 'Golden Empire'

The name *Paphiopedilum* derives from the Greek *Paphos*, an Aegean island with a temple to Aphrodite, the Goddess of Love, and *pedilon*, sandal. Legend has it that one day Aphrodite lost her golden slipper. When a mortal found it and tried to touch it, the slipper was transformed into an exquisite golden orchid. The 60 or so species grow only in Asia, but are similar in appearance to American slipper orchids classified as *Cypripedium* and *Phragmipedium*. Most *Paphiopedilum* species are terrestrial and all have the same distinctive flower with a lip shaped like the toe of a slipper. Their flowers come in many colors and often have stripes, spots, hairs, and warty bumps. The Guinness Book of Records named *Paphiopedilum sanderianum*, a species with pendant side petals nearly three feet long, the world's largest orchid flower.

Opposite: *Paphiopedilum* hybrids

PAPHIOPEDILUM

Top: *Paphiopedilum* Oeno-superbiens Bottom: *Paphiopedilum* Starr Search

Phaius comes from the Greek word *phaios*, grey, and probably refers to the flowers darkening with age or damage. They are commonly called nun's cap orchids because the delicate flowers resemble a nun's headdress. This genus includes about 50 mostly terrestrial species that are found in a variety of habitats and altitudes in parts of Africa, southern Asia and Australia. They were among the first Asian orchids introduced in England, brought back from China by Dr. John Fothergill in 1778. They are generally easy to grow in moist, shady situations and are becoming popular outdoor garden plants in warmer areas of the United States such as Florida.

Opposite: *Phaius* Micro Burst

PHAIUS

Moth Orchid

The name *Phalaenopsis* comes from the Greek *phalaina*, moth, and *opsis*, appearance. Many people are familiar with the popular, large, white-flowered variety that resembles a moth in flight. These mostly epiphytic orchids come from South Asia, the Philippines, Borneo, New Guinea, and Australia and were first described by the Dutch botanist Karl Ludwig Blume in the early 1800s. They grow in hot, steamy lowland forests and need warm, humid conditions to thrive. There are roughly 50 species of *Phalaenopsis* and countless hybrids. Because their flowers are large and long lasting, they have become one of the most popular of all florist crops. Orchid breeders have developed dozens of new and different color forms: flowers in shades of red, peach, green, and yellow, with stripes, spots, and other patterns.

Opposite: *Phalaenopsis* Golden Peoker 'BL' x (Rousserole x Chingruey's Spot)

PHALAENOPSIS

Clockwise from top left: *Phalaenopsis* (Golden Bells x Okay Seven) 'Pine Ridge', *Phalaenopsis* Center Stage 'Penny',
Phalaenopsis Haur Jin Diamond x Black Rose, *Phalaenopsis* Ever-spring King 'Orchis'

Phalaenopsis (Mary Stripes x Paul Tater) 'Pine Ridge'   53

Phragmipedium comes from the Greek for partition, *phragma*, and *pedilon*, slipper, referring to the partitioned ovary and the slipper-shaped lip. There are roughly 20 species of *Phragmipedium* ranging from Central to South America. They can be epiphytic, lithophytic, or terrestrial, but all like very moist conditions. New species and hybrids in shades of red, yellow, and pink are now being introduced into the horticultural trade. Like *Paphiopedilum*, some species have long, pendulous, twisted side petals.

Opposite: *Phragmipedium* besseae hybrids

PHRAGMIPEDIUM

In 1837 an orchid with big blue flowers was discovered in the hills of northern India. It was named *Vanda caerulea* and caused a sensation when it was sent to England. *Vanda*, Sanskrit for this type of orchid, is a widespread genus of 40 epiphytic species that grow from the Himalayas through tropical Asia and into northern Australia and can range from miniatures to large plants more than five feet tall. Their long stems carry fans of fleshy leaves and masses of white cord-like roots. Like their closely related cousins, *Ascocentrum*, they are one of the few orchids that come in all colors of the rainbow and are often fragrant. Thousands of cultivated forms come in shades of purple, blue, orange, apricot, yellow, and red.

Opposite: *Vanda* Savina Pagel

VANDA

Vandaceous orchids, *Epidendrum* hybrids

Clockwise from top left: x *Vascostylis* Viboon Velvet 'Powder Puff', x *Aranda* Noorah Alsagoff , *Vanda* Tokyo Blue 'Indigo', *Vanda* Robert's Delight 'Fuchsia Fantasy'

Growing Orchids at Home

Orchids make wonderful, long-lived houseplants that will flower regularly with proper care.
The key to their cultivation is to make certain that you select and site your orchids appropriately.
Keep in mind that, depending on the species, orchids come from areas that range from sea level
to sub-alpine mountaintops, but that generally experience a drop in nighttime temperatures.
Orchids are therefore horticulturally divided into three categories:

Warm Growers	Intermediate Growers	Cool Growers
Daytime temperature: 75° and up *Nighttime temperature: 70°*	*Daytime temperature: 65° - 75°* *Nighttime temperature: 60°*	*Daytime temperature: 55° - 65°* *Nighttime temperature: 50°*
Cattleya	Cattleya	Cymbidium
Dendrobium	Dendrobium	Dendrobium
Epidendrum	Epidendrum	Miltoniopsis
Oncidium	Oncidium	Odontoglossum
Paphiopedilum	Miltoniopsis	
Phaius	Paphiopedilum	
Phalaenopsis	Phragmipedium	
Vanda		

Appropriate light levels are very important to ensure that your orchids thrive and flower well. Most prefer bright light, but not direct sun, as in an east window or in a spot a short distance from a south or west window. Direct sunlight will scorch the leaves of most types of orchids; light levels in bright windows can be tempered by blinds, sheer curtains, or shades. Shade-loving orchids such as *Paphiopedilum* and *Ludisia* will grow happily in a bright north window or a slightly shaded east window. Full-sun lovers such as vandas should be placed directly in a south or west window; they will not reliably flower unless they are grown in that exposure.

Watering is another very significant factor. Orchids are mainly killed by "kindness" through over-watering. Take into consideration that epiphytic orchids naturally grow attached to tree branches with excellent drainage and air circulation around their roots. To duplicate these conditions, orchids are usually grown in a fairly open mixture of bark, perlite, and charcoal. Some orchids may also be grown directly mounted on a piece of wood, a slab of tree fern fiber, or cork. With a few exceptions, orchids should not be planted in potting soil. Terrestrial orchids should be grown in soil that is very loose and well-drained, and amended with bark or perlite. Weekly watering will generally suffice for most plants, however one should always pay close attention to individual specimens — test the media with your finger to determine whether or not your plant is in need of water — if the potting mix feels damp just below its surface, don't water!

Proper fertilization is fairly easy to accomplish. Orchids thrive on a steady, weak stream of nutrients. The best way to provide this is to make a 1/4 strength solution of a regular, balanced, houseplant fertilizer (say 10-10-10, or 14-14-14) and use this every time you water. Remember the phrase "weakly-weekly" when fertilizing and your orchids will thrive.

Direct sunlight may fade orchid flowers. Make certain that you don't spray water on the blossoms when sun is on them as this may cause pinhole burns and scorching. Keeping flowers away from hot, dry air will make them last longer. If your air is very dry, set the plant on a pebble-filled tray with water added to just below the bottom of the pot.

Some orchid flowers survive longer than others: cattleyas usually stay fresh for 1-2 weeks, while some *Phalaenopsis* and *Oncidium* hybrids may last for 3 months or more. A common question is: "What do I do when the flowers die?" With only a few exceptions, the flower stem should be severed with a clean sharp knife about a half-inch from its base. *Phalaenopsis* may sometimes produce a second, smaller spike on the same stem, but this tends to offer less spectacular flowers and may compromise the next season's flowering, so it is usually best to remove the main spike once it has faded.

Here is a short list of some of the easier orchids for home growing.

Cattleya Clear Morn

Vanda Tokyo Blue 'Indigo'

Phalaenopsis
Ever Spring Prince 'Pretty Cat'

CATTLEYA

Large, flamboyant, often fragrant, but comparatively short-lived blooms.
CARE: *Warm to intermediate temperatures, bright indirect light.*

CYMBIDIUM

Sturdy spikes of waxy, corsage-type flowers, handsome strap-leaved clumps of foliage.
CARE: *Cool temperatures necessary to flower.*

DENDROBIUM

Colorful flowers on cane-like stems.
CARE: *Warm temperatures for the cane-type species and hybrids, bright sun.*

ONCIDIUM

Sprays of colorful, long-lasting, small flowers.
CARE: *Warm to intermediate temperatures, bright indirect light.*

PHALAENOPSIS

Elegant, long-lived sprays of moth-like flowers. Probably the best orchid for a beginner.
CARE: *Warm temperatures, moderate light.*

PAPHIOPEDILUM

Exotic, long-lasting, slipper-like flowers that bloom one-at-a-time.
CARE: *Warm to intermediate temperatures, shady conditions found in a north window.*

PHRAGMIPEDIUM

Exotic, slipper-like flowers in shades of green, white, beige, yellow, pink, and red bloom successively over a long period.
CARE: *Warm to intermediate temperatures, thrives with abundant water.*

VANDA

Large, flat, open flowers, often with checkered patterns.
CARE: *Warm temperatures, full, direct sunlight and frequent watering.*

Every year the Shop in the Garden presents an extensive selection of fine orchids for sale. These range from the easy-to-care-for varieties mentioned above to less common orchids that are hard-to-find collectors' dreams. Be sure to visit the shop during *The Orchid Show* to make your orchid experience complete.

Pronunciation Guide

ANGULOA an-gyoo-LOW-ah

ANGRAECUM an-GRY-kum

CATTLEYA KAT-lee-ya

CYMBIDIUM sim-BID-ee-um

DENDROBIUM den-DRO-bee-um

EPIDENDRUM eh-pee-DEN-drum

HOULLETIA hoo-LET-ee-ah

LUDISIA loo-DIS-ee-ah

MILTONIA mil-TONE-ee-ah

MILTONIOPSIS mil-tone-ee-OP-sis

ODONTOGLOSSUM oh-dont-oh-GLOS-um

ONCIDIUM on-SID-ee-um

PAPHIOPEDILUM paf-ee-oh-PED-i-lum

PHAIUS FAY-us

PHALAENOPSIS fail-eh-NOP-sis

PHRAGMIPEDIUM frag-mi-PEE-dee-um

PSYCHOPSIS sye-KOP-sis

RENANTHERA ren-AN-ther-a

VANDA VAN-da

ZYGOPETALUM zy-go-PET-a-lum

Acknowledgments

Text by Kenneth M. Cameron, Ph.D.,
Associate Curator and Director of the Lewis B. and Dorothy Cullman Program for Molecular Systematics Studies and Darrin Duling, *Curator of Glasshouse Collections.*

Edited by Margaret Falk,
Marc Hachadourian,
and JoAnn Kawell.

Special thanks to Francisca Coelho,
Director of the Enid A. Haupt Conservatory,
and to the Conservatory staff for their indispensable help in setting up and maintaining the show each year.

Published by Shop in the Garden Books
The New York Botanical Garden
Bronx River Parkway at Fordham Road
Bronx, NY 10458

www.nybgShopintheGarden.org

Developed by Shop in the Garden Books:

Catherine Hipp
Director of Garden Retail and Business Development

Ellen Bruzelius
Associate Director of Business Development

Produced in association with Patrick Filley Associates, Inc.

Design by Salsgiver Coveney Associates Inc.

Printed in Hong Kong
ISBN 0-89327-963-3

Proceeds from the sale of this book support
The New York Botanical Garden.

Photographs:

Front cover:
x Doritaenopsis Formosa Beauty x (Minho Valentine x Taisuco Firebird),
x Wilsonara Lisa Devos 'HOF #6'

Page 1:
Angraecum sesquipedale (Darwin's star orchid)

Frontispiece:
Howeara Lava Burst 'Puanani'

Back cover:
Cymbidium Winter Bride 'BVF 18198'